THE
UKULELE
HOLIDAY COLLECTION

WWW.BRENTROBITAILLE.COM

KALYMI MUSIC

OTHER BOOKS BY BRENT ROBITAILLE

Celtic Collection for Ukulele
Ukulele Blank Tab Collection and Reference Book
The Pop Rock Looper Pedal Book
The Blues Guitar Looper Pedal Book
Standard Guitar Tuning - Celtic Collection
Open D Guitar Tuning - Celtic Collection
Open G Guitar Tuning - Celtic Collection
Improve Your Guitar Chord Playing
Slide Guitar Collection
Celtic Collection Fiddle - Tab & Notes
Holiday Collection for Fiddle - Tab & Notes
Traditional Collection Fiddle - Tab & Notes
Fiddle Tab - Celtic Collection
Celtic Collection for Mandolin
The Complete Cigar Box Guitar Chord Book
Cigar Box Guitar - Jazz & Blues Unlimited Book One & Two
Cigar Box Guitar Blues Overload
101 Riffs for Cigar Box Guitar
Celtic Collection for Cigar Box Guitar
The Ultimate Collection – How to Play Cigar Box Guitar Vol. 1 & 2
Cigar Box Guitar - The Technique Book
Holiday Collection for Cigar Box Guitar

Recordings - Ebooks - Sheet Music
Available at:

www.brentrobitaille.com

KALYMI MUSIC

PUBLISHED BY KALYMI MUSIC
©2020 Kalymi Music

Introduction

The Ukulele Christmas Songbook has thirty of the most loved holiday favourites arranged for beginner to intermediate ukulelists. Each song is shown in lead sheet format, meaning the melody, lyrics, and chords are included. The melodies have both ukulele tablature and notation, and each song includes chord diagrams showing the finger placement. Twenty songs have a more advanced fingerstyle arrangement for players looking for a fuller-sounding chord melody with chords and melody together.

There is also a useful 30+ page ukulele reference section for players wishing to expand their ukulele knowledge. This reference section includes a chord library of the most common ukulele chords, strumming and fingerpicking patterns, chord and arpeggio fingerboard diagrams in every key, and a collection of ukulele scales and scale patterns to warm-up your fingers.

Visit my website to hear some audio tracks and browse other ukulele books and arrangements from Kalymi Music.

www.brentrobitaille.com

or

www.kalymimusic.com

CONTENTS

30 CHRISTMAS SONGS

UKULELE REFERENCE SECTION

HOW TO READ TABLATURE (TAB)

To read tablature, you need to know four things:

1) What string is the note on? - Strings are thin (1st) to thick (3rd) then thin (4th).
2) What fret is the note on? - Fret numbers are left to right.
3) Which finger do I use? - Keep all fingers in position (1-2-3-4) where possible
   when playing single notes, and most comfortable fingerings for chords.
4) How long to let the note ring? - Based on the song's rhythm but generally
   keep fingers on fretboard as long as possible to let notes ring throughout.

Fingerboard Number Chart

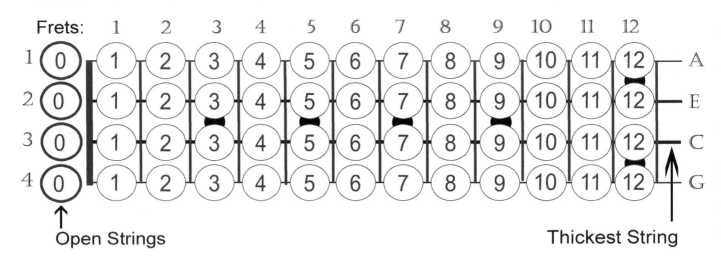

Examples:

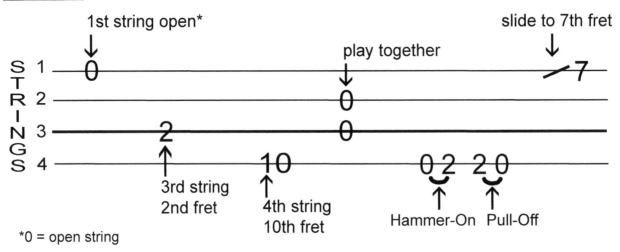

*0 = open string

HOW TO READ CHORD DIAGRAMS

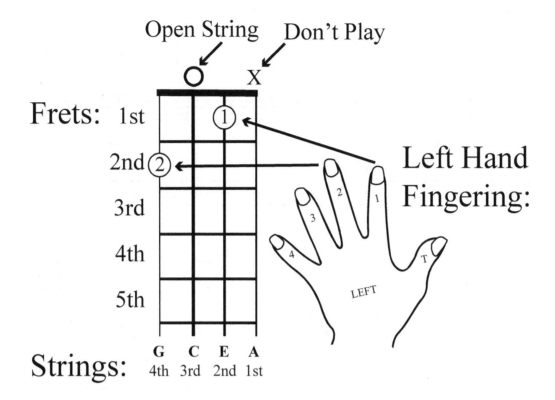

Barre Chords

Barre chords require covering several strings with one finger. In this example, place your 1st finger on strings 1 to 4 on the second fret then add the 2nd and 3rd finger to form the G major chord.

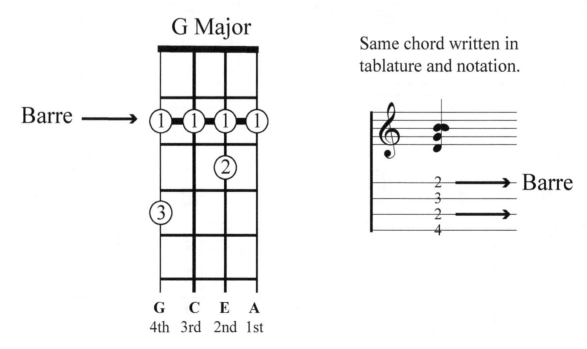

ALL THROUGH THE NIGHT

ALL THROUGH THE NIGHT

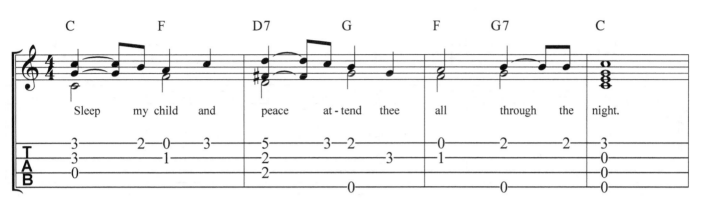

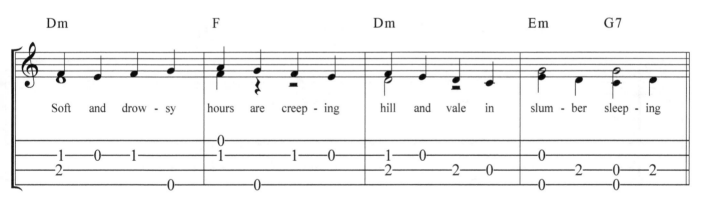

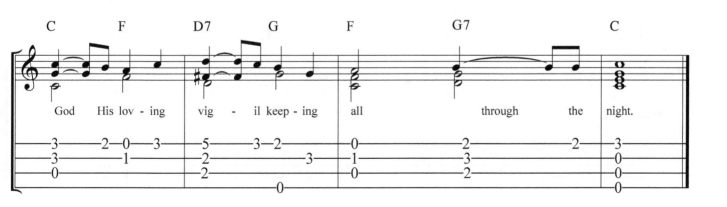

ANGELS WE HAVE HEARD ON HIGH

ANGELS WE HAVE HEARD ON HIGH

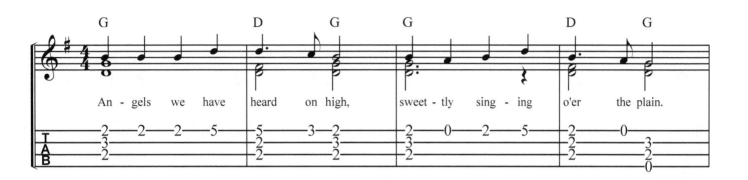

An - gels we have heard on high, sweet - ly sing - ing o'er the plain.

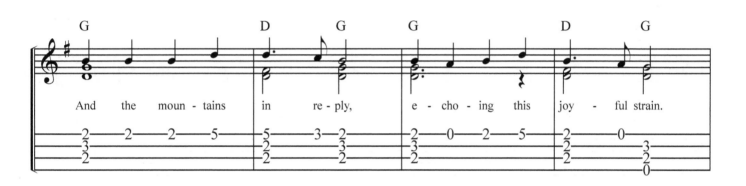

And the moun - tains in re - ply, e - cho - ing this joy - ful strain.

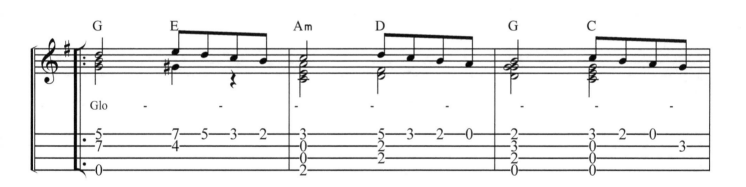

Glo - - - - - - - -

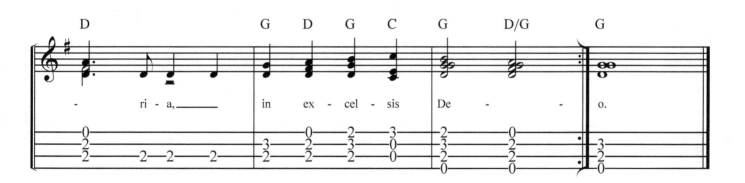

- ri - a,_____ in ex - cel - sis De - - o.

AULD LANG SYNE

AULD LANG SYNE

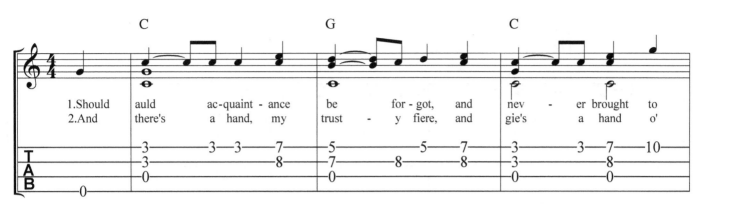

1.Should auld ac-quaint-ance be for-got, and nev-er brought to
2.And there's a hand, my trust-y fiere, and gie's a hand o'

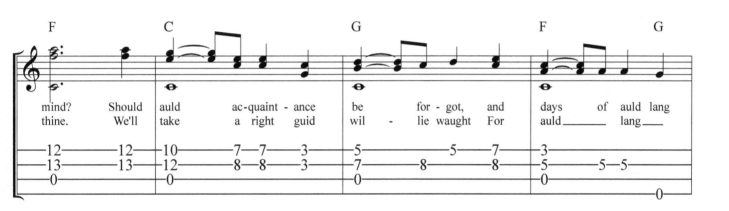

mind? Should auld ac-quaint-ance be for-got, and days of auld lang
thine. We'll take a right guid wil - lie waught For auld_____ lang_____

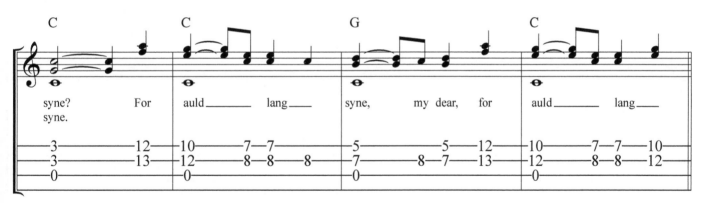

syne? For auld_____ lang_____ syne, my dear, for auld_____ lang_____
syne.

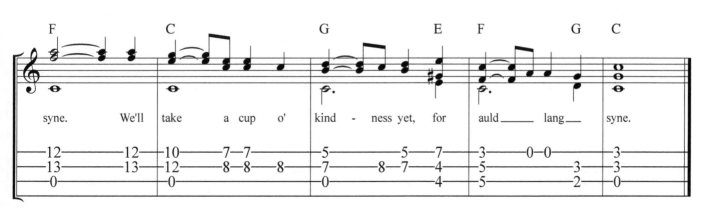

syne. We'll take a cup o' kind - ness yet, for auld_____ lang_____ syne.

AWAY IN THE MANGER

AWAY IN A MANGER

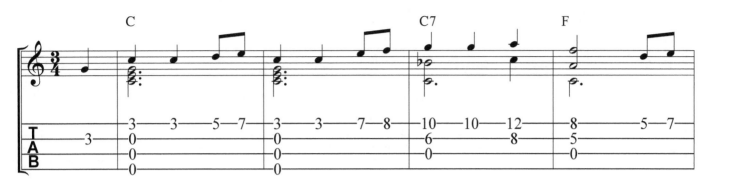

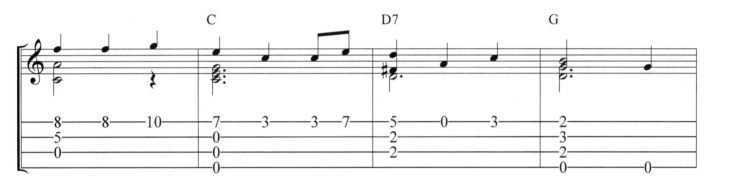

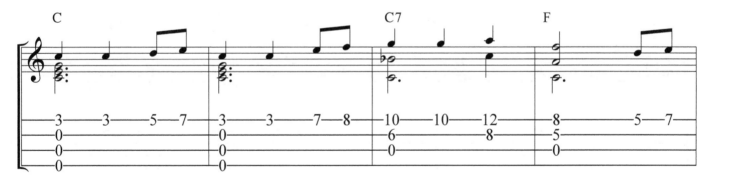

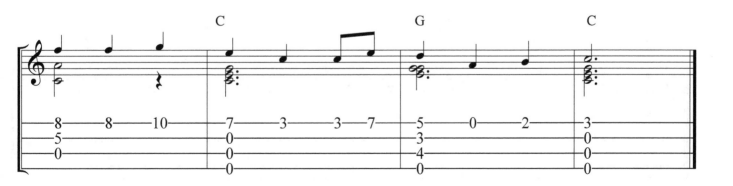

Boar's Head Carol

COVENTRY CAROL

DECK THE HALLS

THE FIRST NOEL

GO TELL IT ON THE MOUNTAIN

GO TELL IT ON THE MOUNTAIN

GOD REST YE MERRY GENTLEMEN

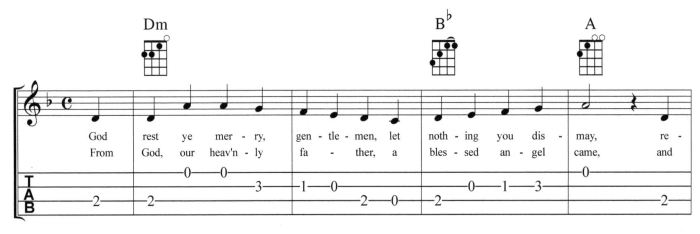

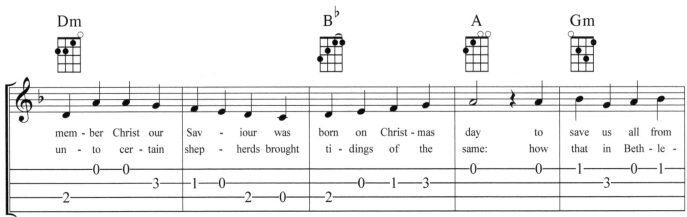

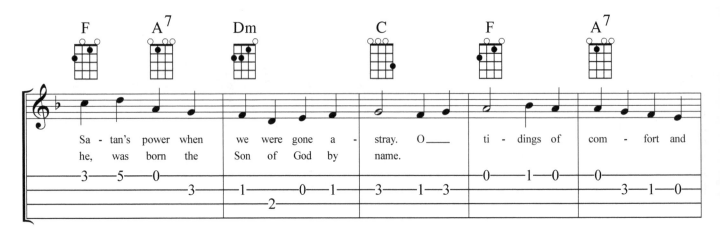

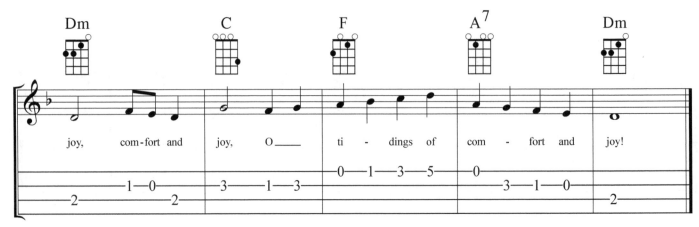

GOD REST YE MERRY GENTLEMEN

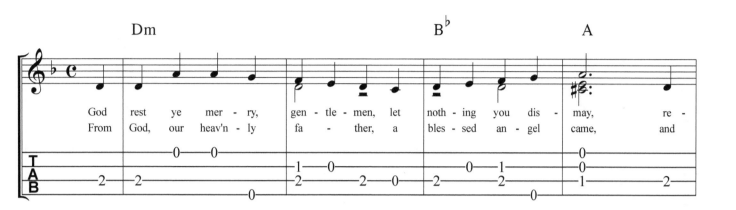

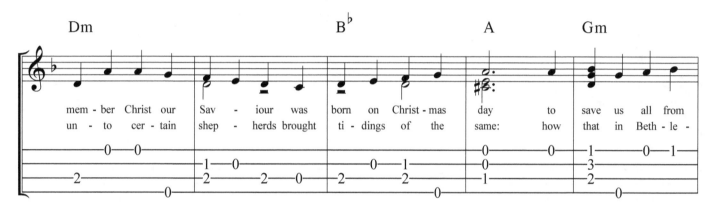

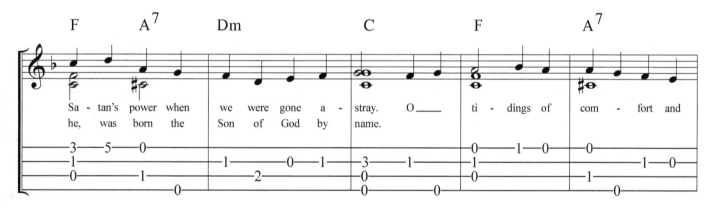

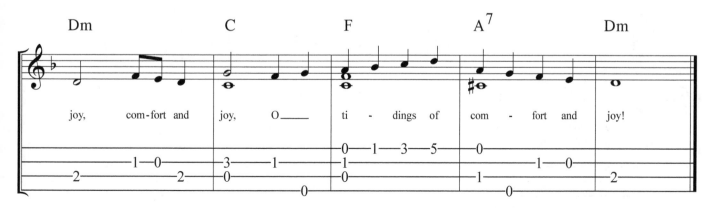

GOOD KING WENCESLAS

GOOD KING WENCESLAS

HARK! THE HERALD ANGELS SING

HARK! THE HERALD ANGELS SING

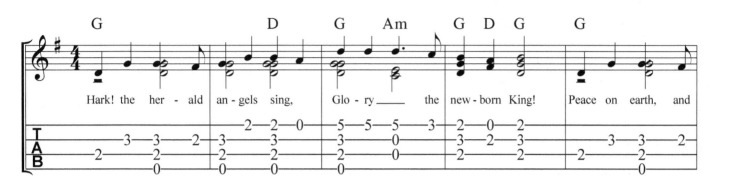

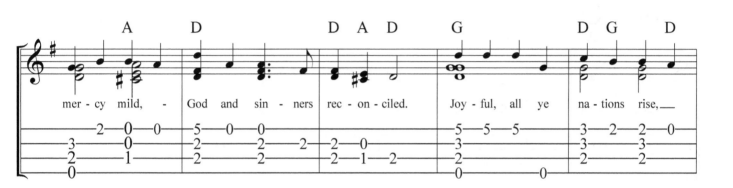

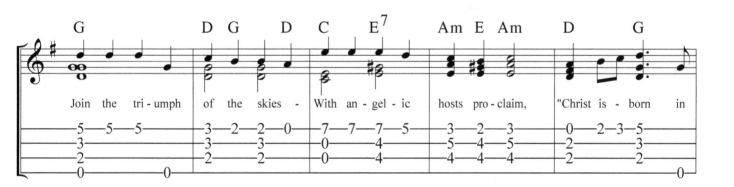

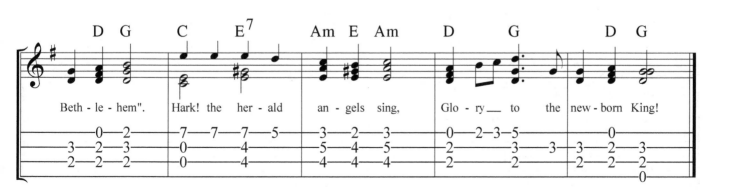

HERE WE COME A CAROLING

HERE WE COME A CAROLING

I SAW THREE SHIPS

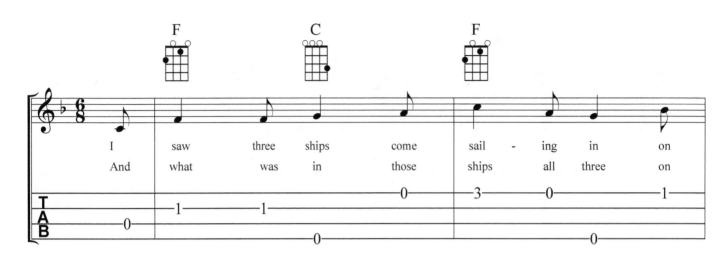

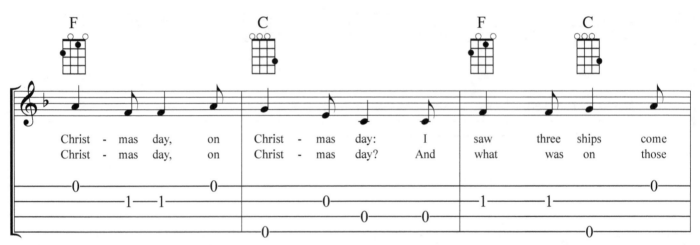

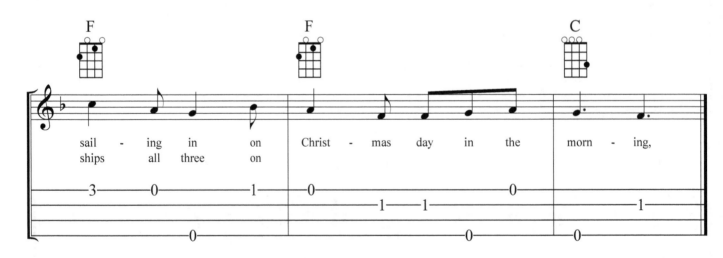

I SAW THREE SHIPS

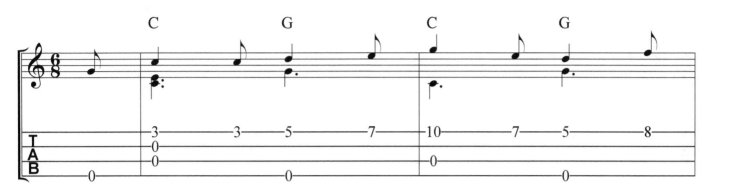

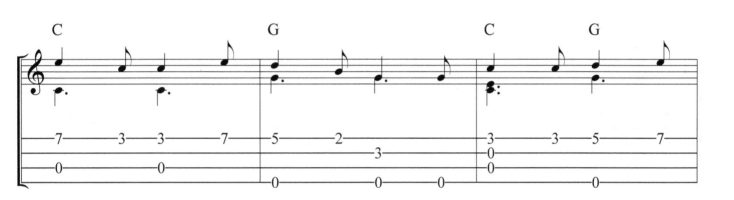

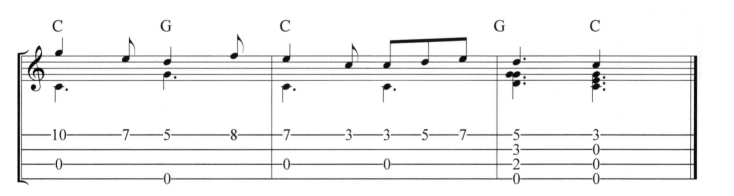

IT CAME UPON THE MIDNIGHT CLEAR

JINGLE BELLS

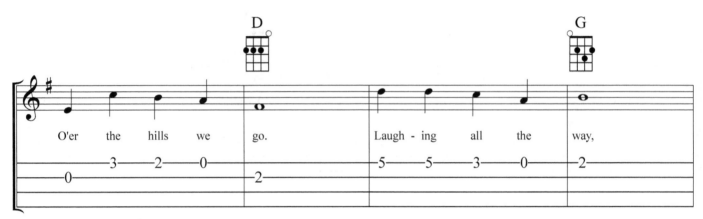

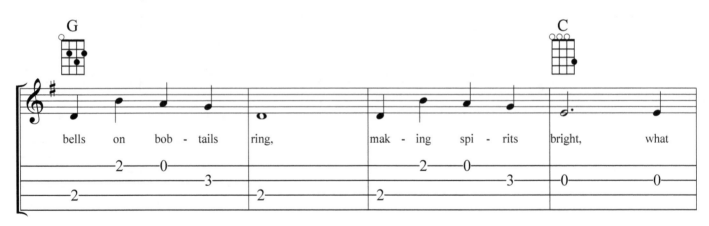

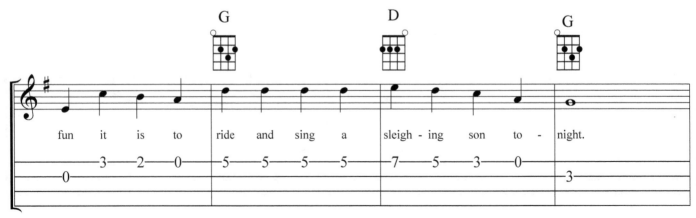

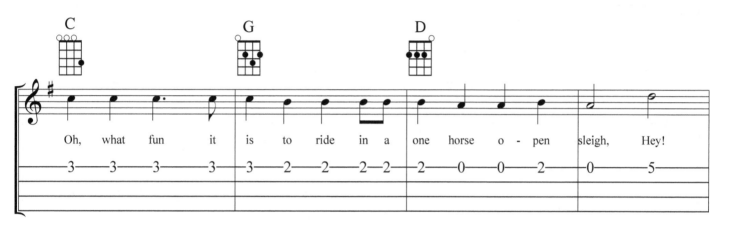

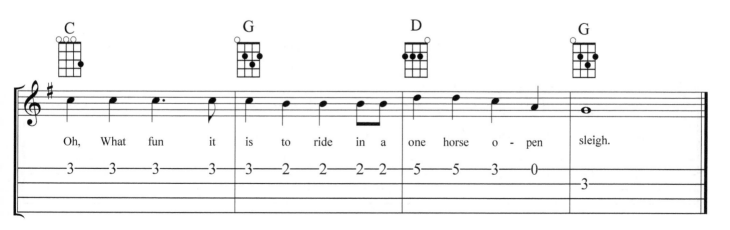

JOLLY OLD ST. NICHOLAS

JOLLY OLD ST. NICHOLAS

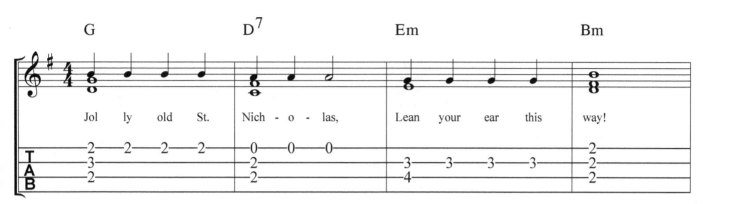

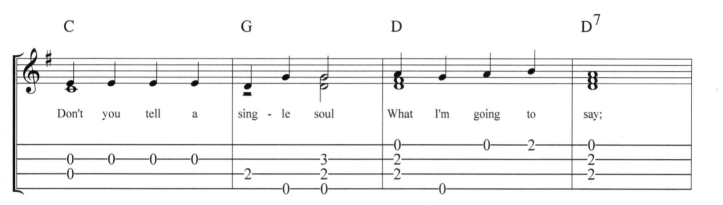

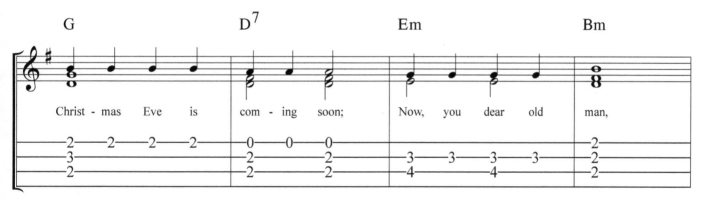

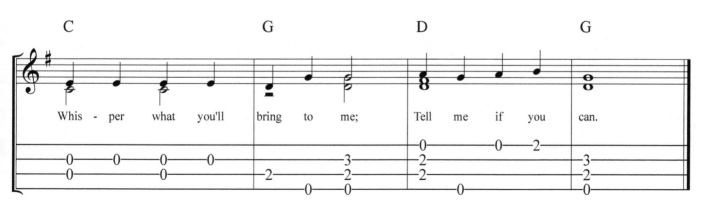

JOY TO THE WORLD

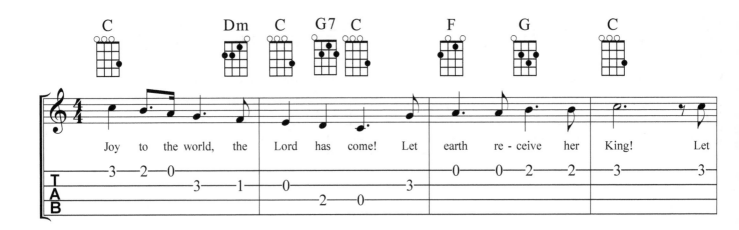

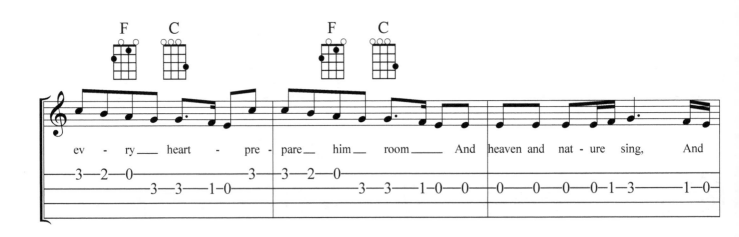

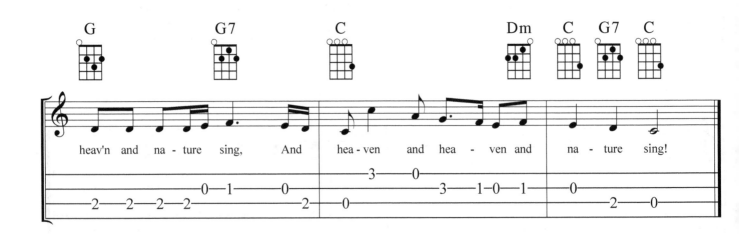

JOY TO THE WORLD

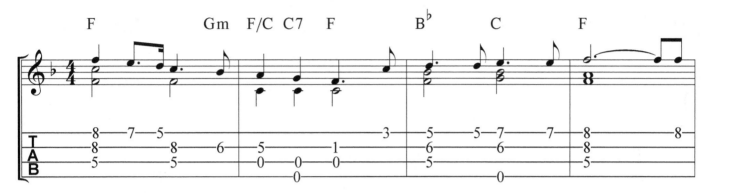

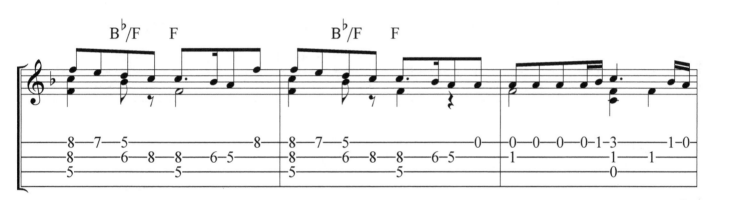

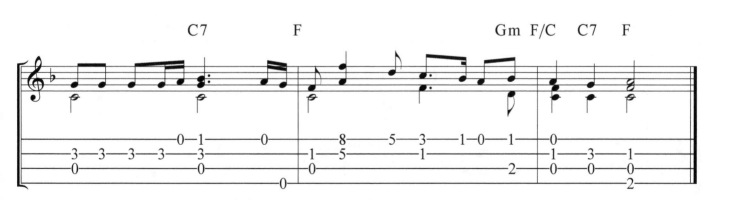

O CHRISTMAS TREE

O CHRISTMAS TREE

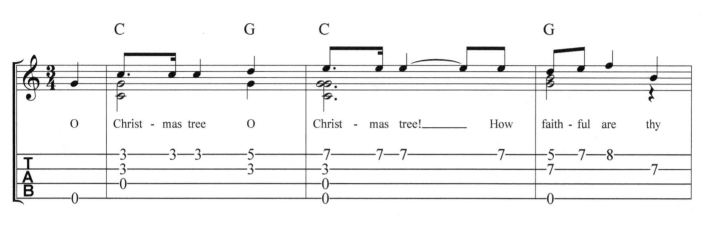

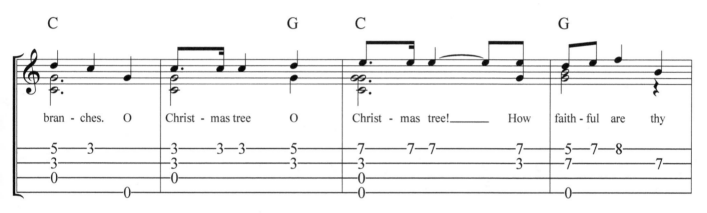

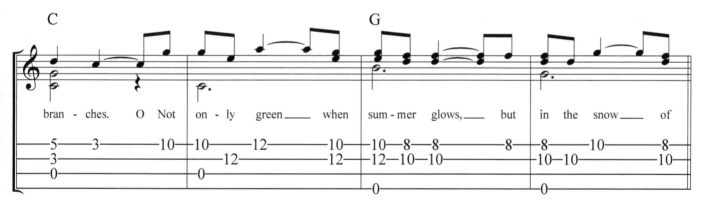

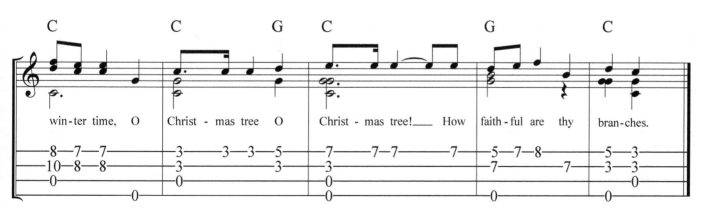

O COME, ALL YE FAITHFUL

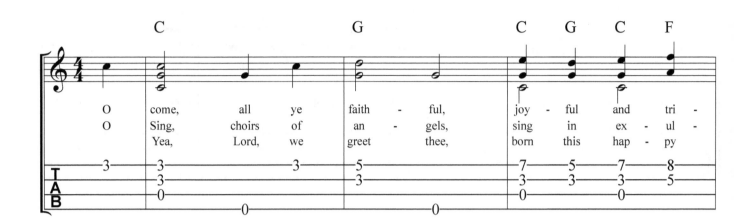

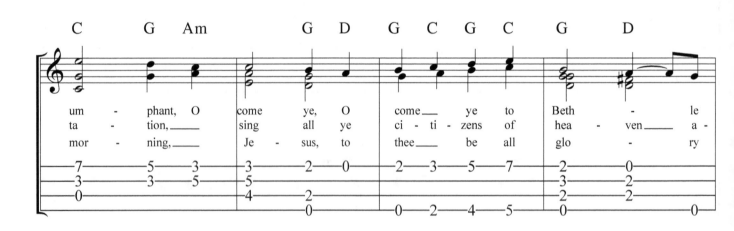

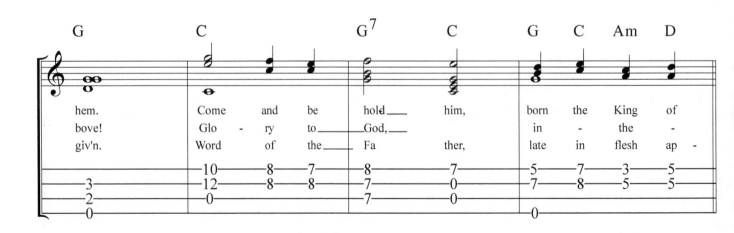

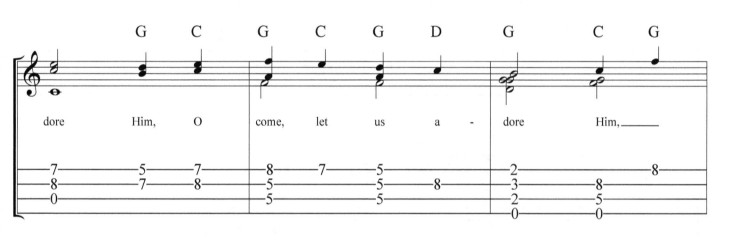

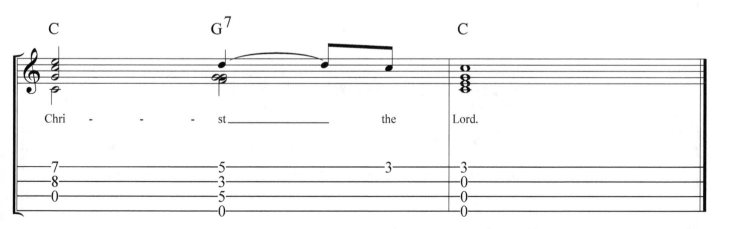

O COME ALL YE FAITHFUL

O COME O COME EMMANUEL

O HOLY NIGHT

O LITTLE TOWN OF BETHLEHEM

O LITTLE TOWN OF BETHLEHEM

SILENT NIGHT

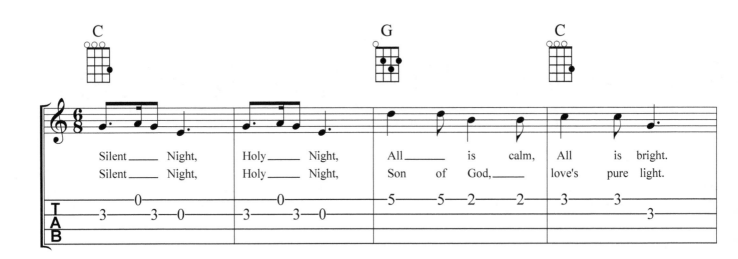

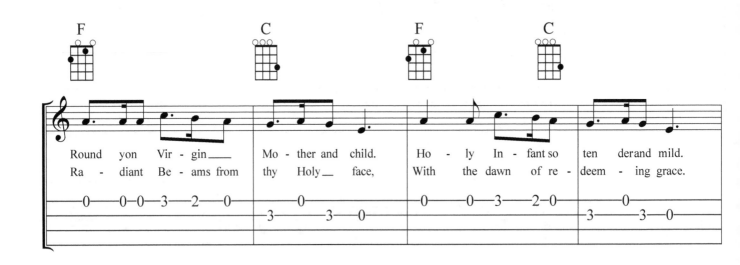

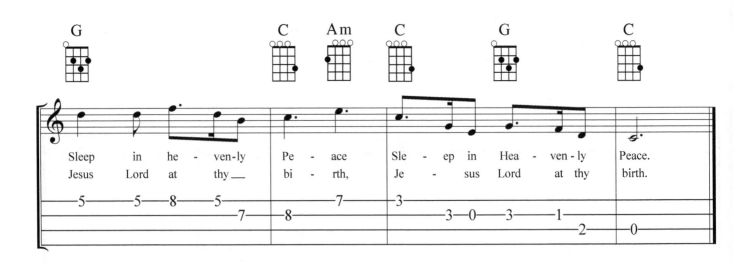

SILENT NIGHT

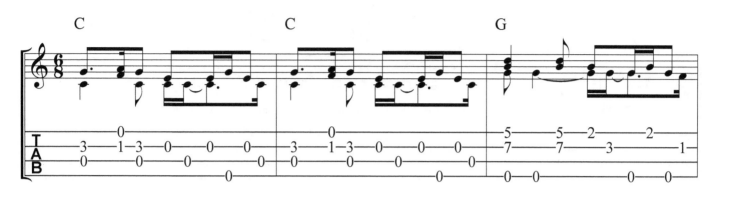

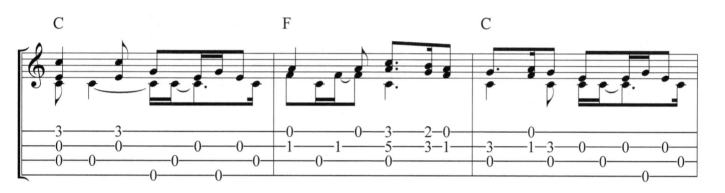

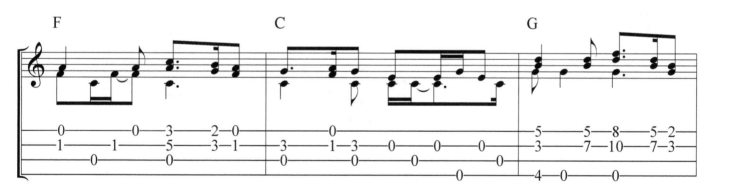

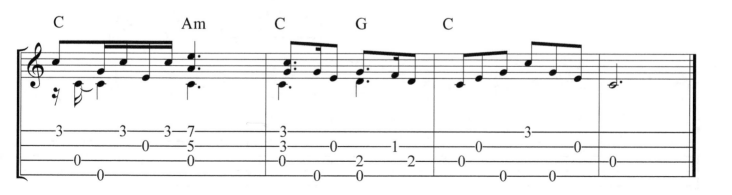

THE TWELVE DAYS OF CHRISTMAS

Additional Lyrics:

6 Geese a Laying
7 Swans a Swimming
8 Maids a Milking

9 Ladies Dancing
10 Lords a Leaping
11 Pipers Piping
12 Drummers Drumming

UP ON THE HOUSETOP

UP ON THE HOUSETOP

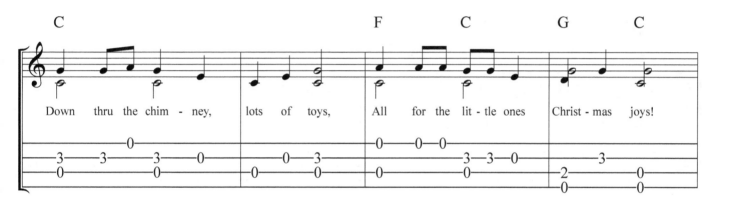

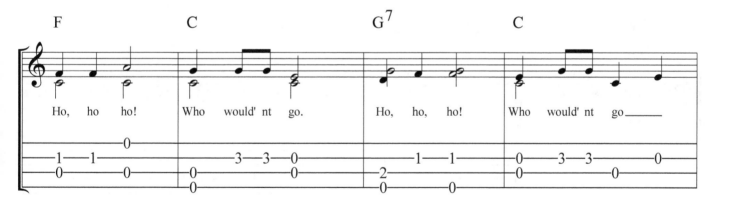

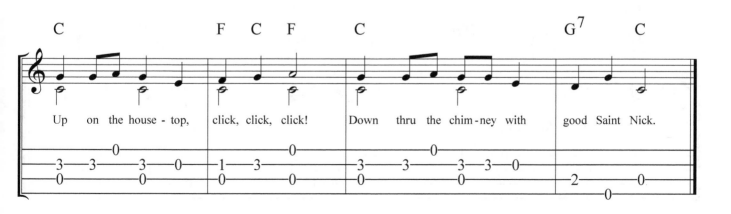

WE THREE KINGS

WE WISH YOU A MERRY CHRISTMAS

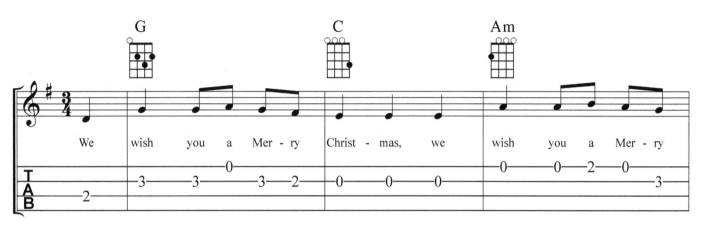

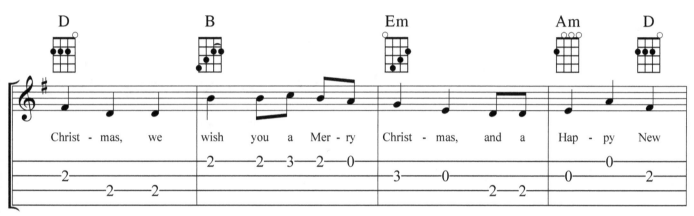

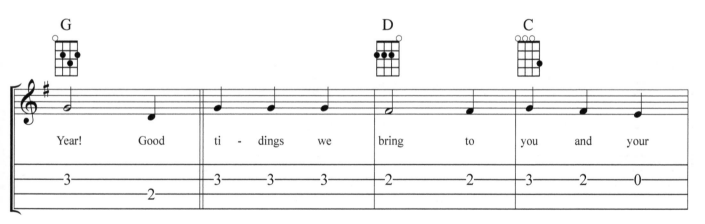

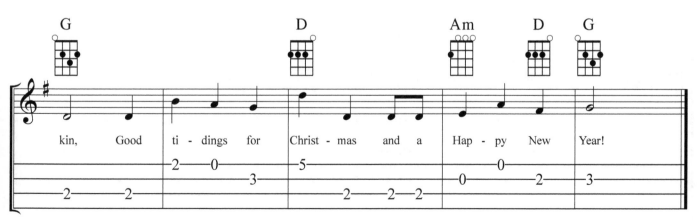

WE WISH YOU A MERRY CHRISTMAS

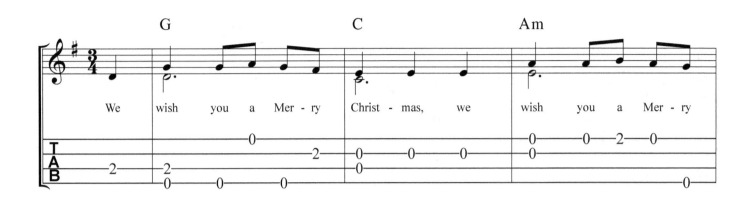

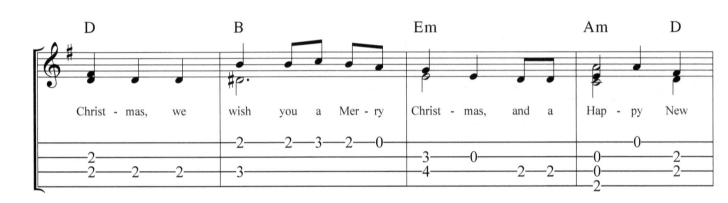

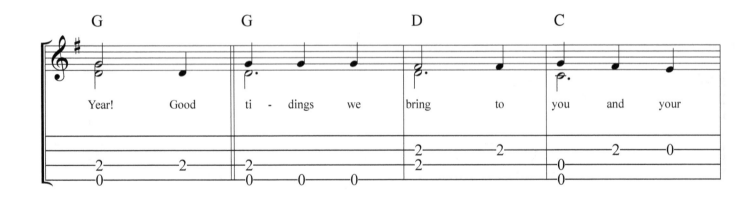

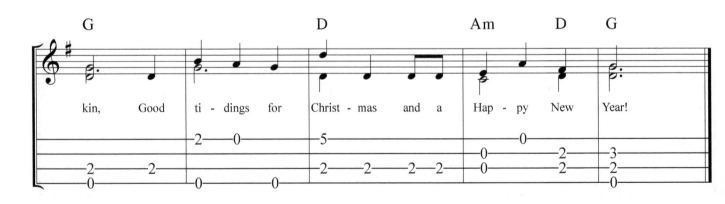

THE WEXFORD CAROL

WHAT CHILD IS THIS?

WHAT CHILD IS THIS?

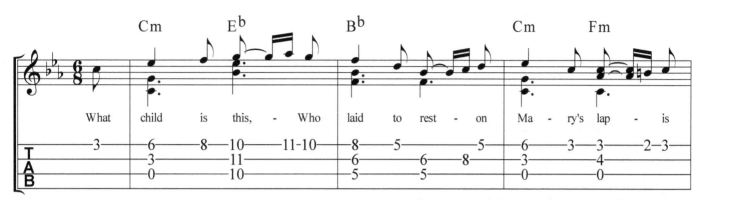

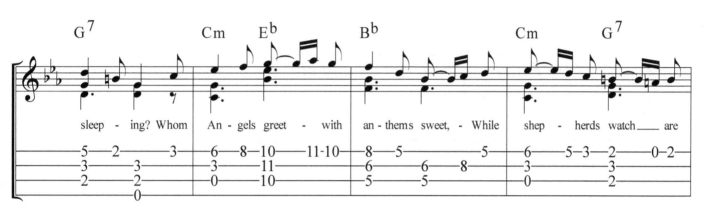

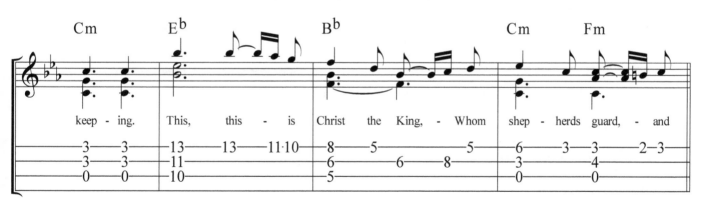

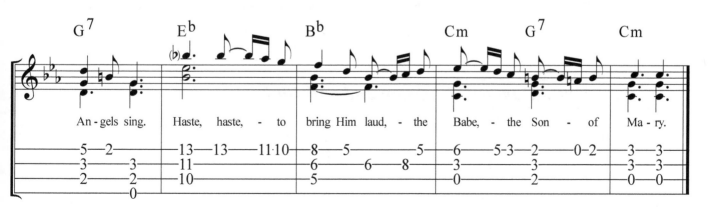

STRUMMING PATTERNS - BASICS

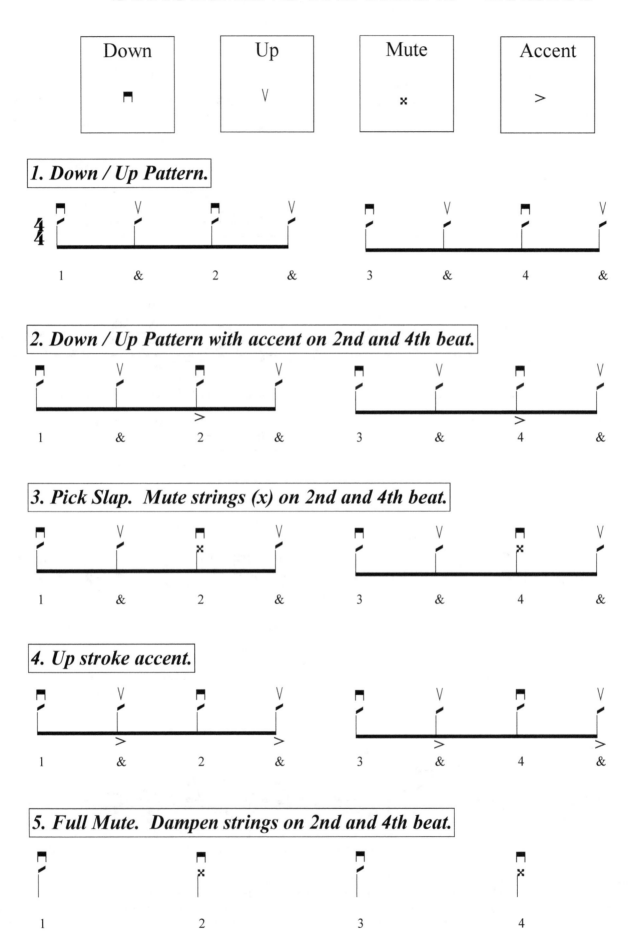

STRUMMING PATTERNS IN: 3/4 - 6/8 - 4/4

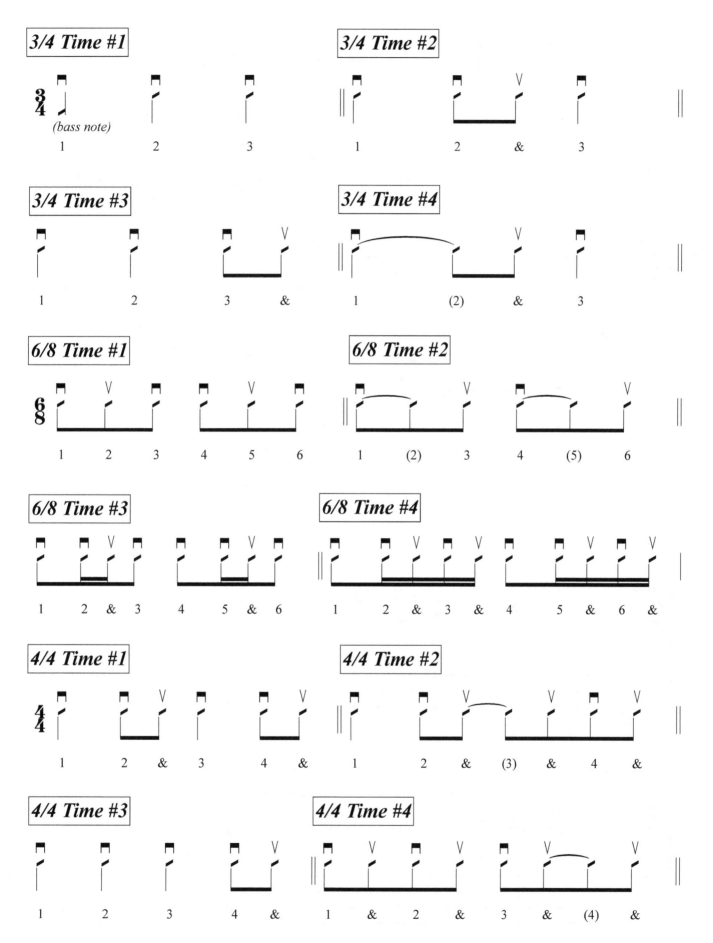

UKULELE FINGERPICKING PATTERNS

Here are some fingerpicking patterns you can apply to the songs in the book. The letters under the notes are for the right hand fingpicking patterns: **T = Thumb, I = Index, M = Middle.**

Thumb - Finger Strum   **Thumb - Down Up Finger Strum**

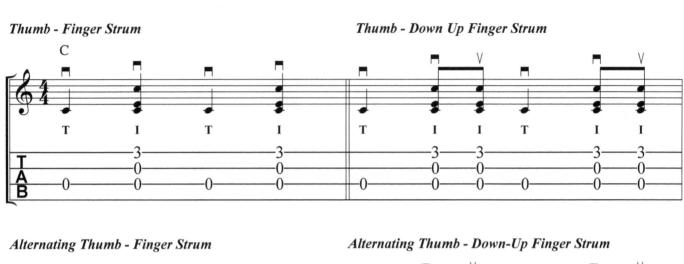

Alternating Thumb - Finger Strum   **Alternating Thumb - Down-Up Finger Strum**

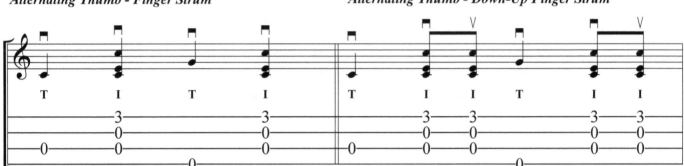

Thumb Double Pluck Fingers

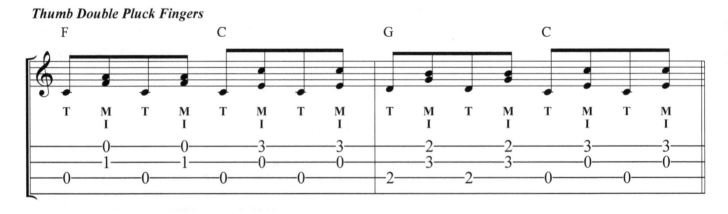

Travis Picking #1   **Travis Picking #2**

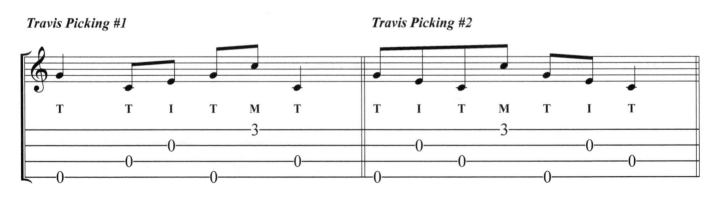

Travis Picking #3 - Pinch   *Travis Picking #4 - Double Pinch*

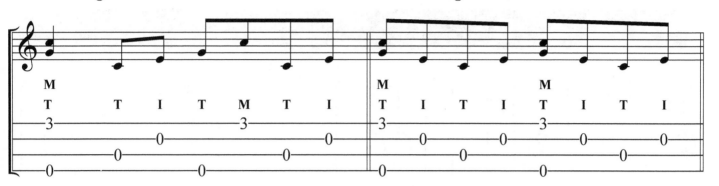

Forward Roll   *Backward Roll*

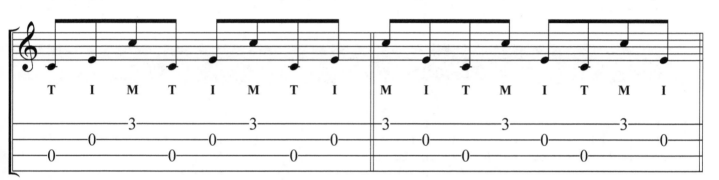

3/4 Time #1   *3/4 Time #2*   *3/4 Time #3*

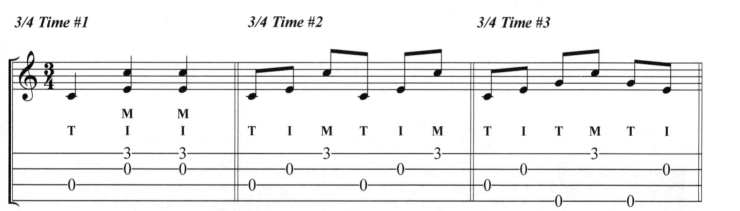

6/8 Time #1   *6/8 Time #2*   *6/8 Time #3*

MAJOR CHORDS

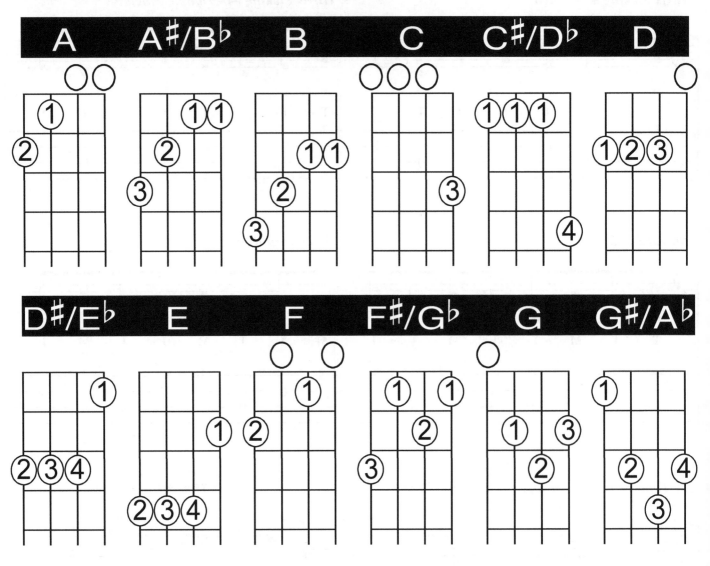

MINOR CHORDS

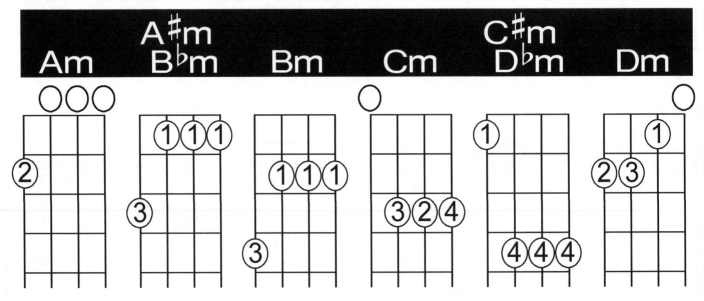

MINOR CHORDS

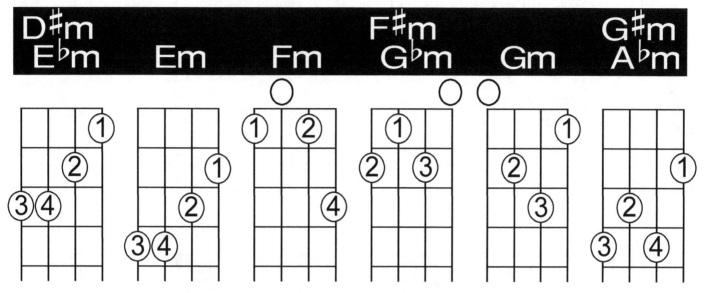

DOMINANT 7th CHORDS

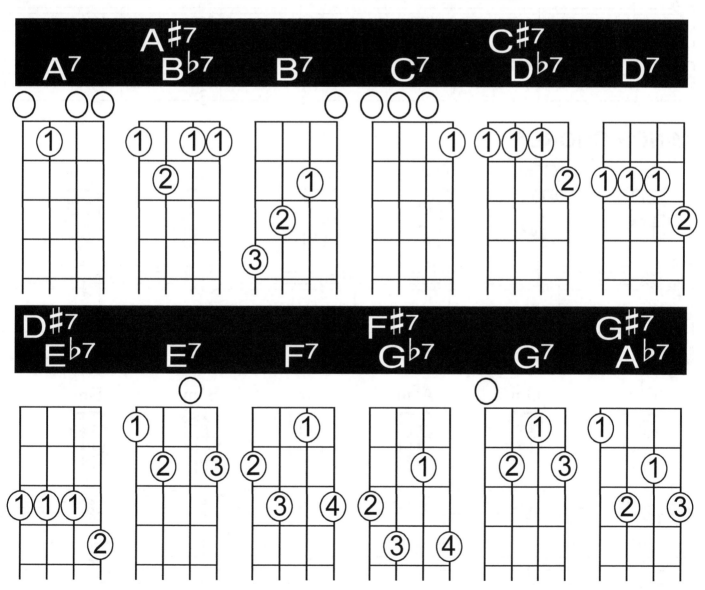

MAJOR CHORDS

MINOR CHORDS

DOMINANT 7th CHORDS

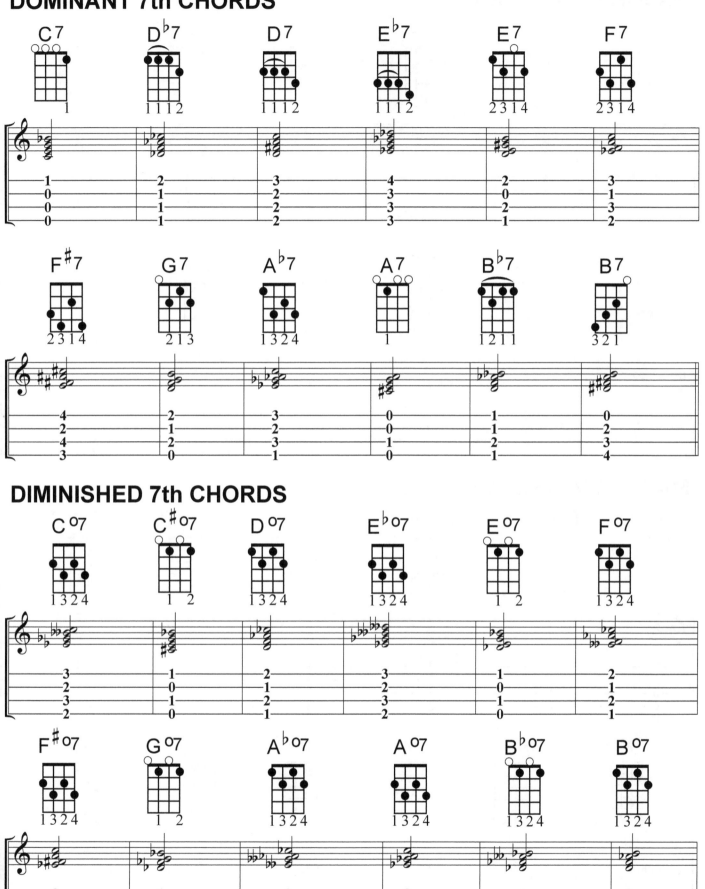

DIMINISHED 7th CHORDS

MAJOR 6th CHORDS

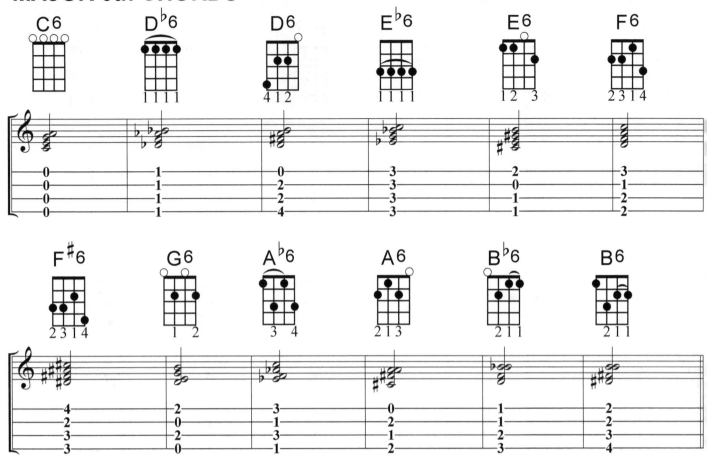

MAJOR 7th CHORDS

MINOR 7th CHORDS

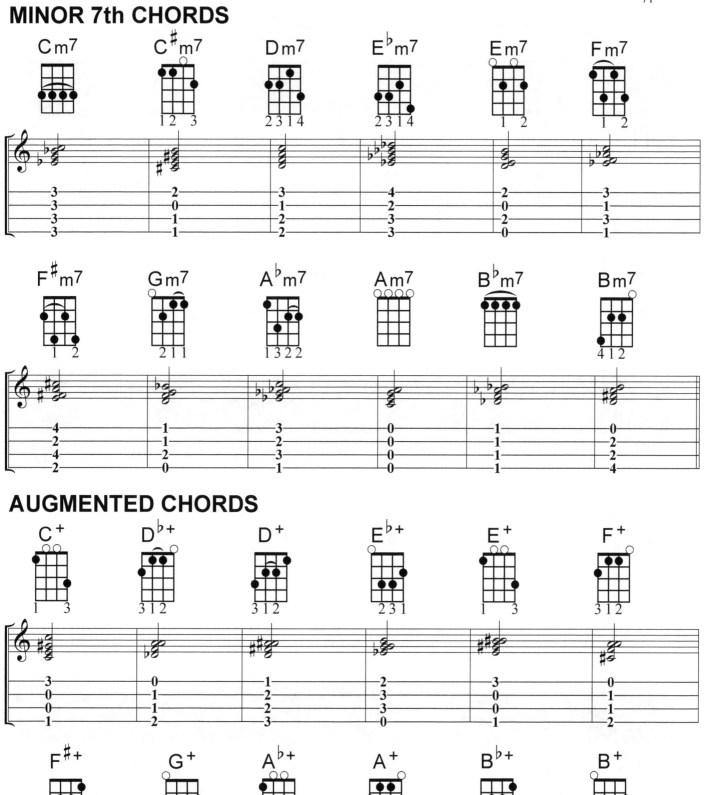

AUGMENTED CHORDS

CHORDS & ARPEGGIOS - A

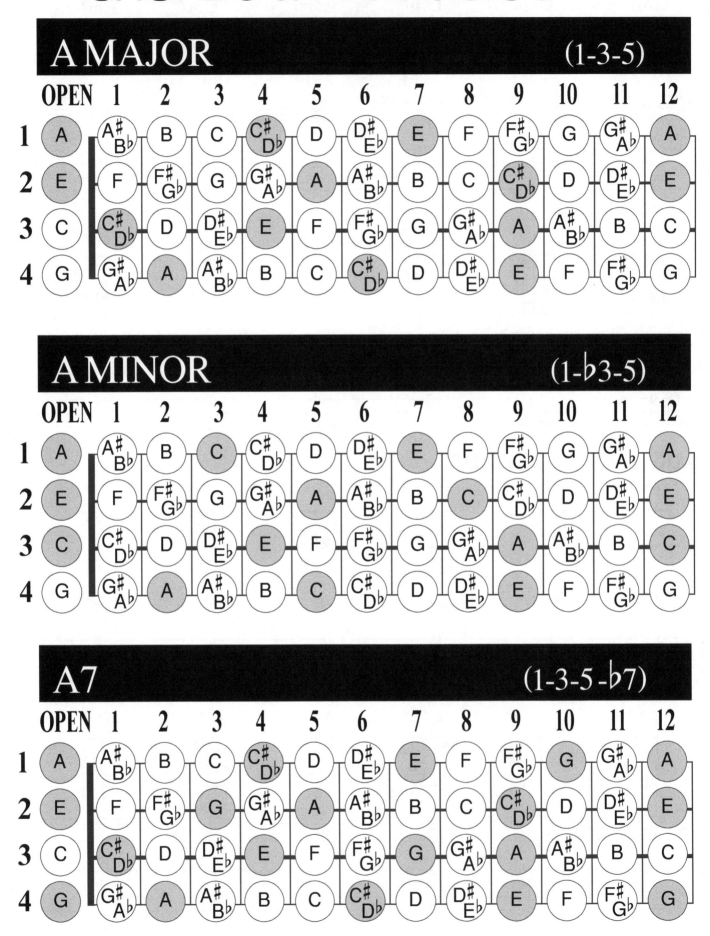

CHORDS & ARPEGGIOS - B♭

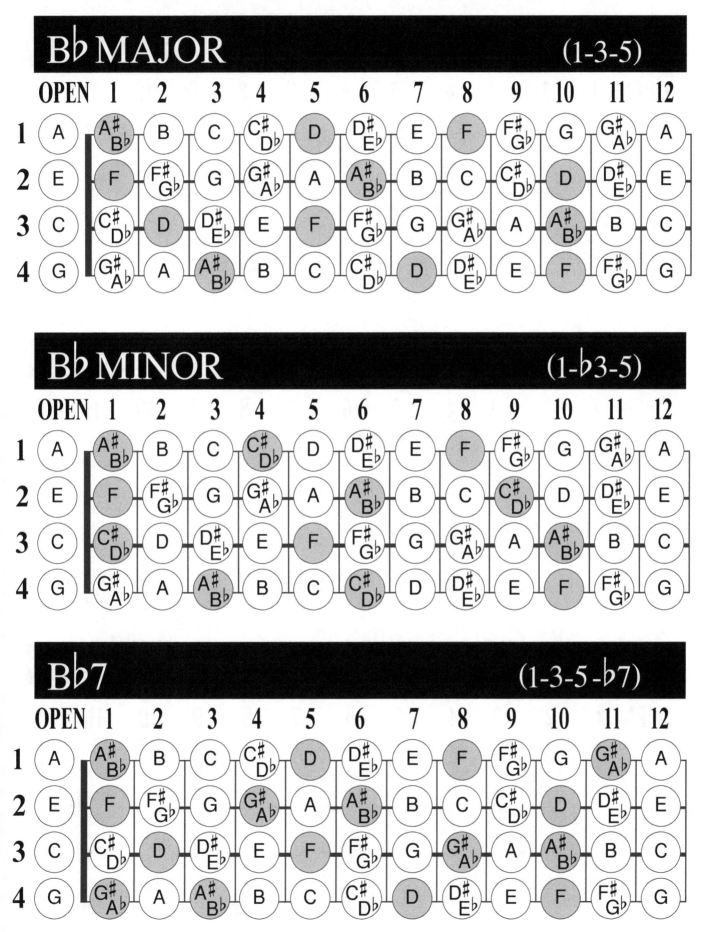

CHORDS & ARPEGGIOS - B

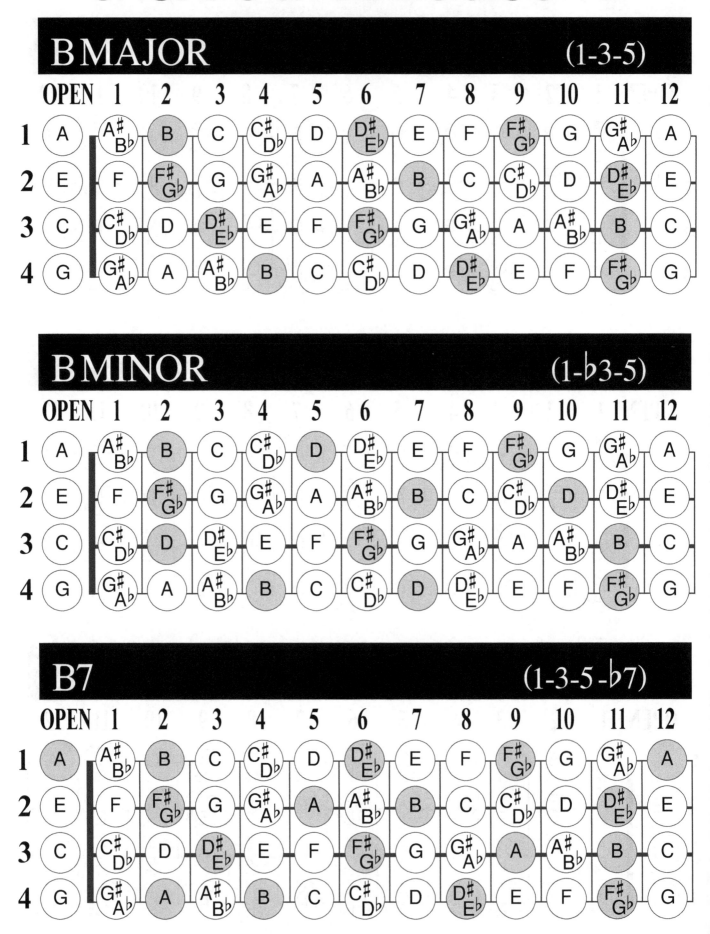

CHORDS & ARPEGGIOS - C

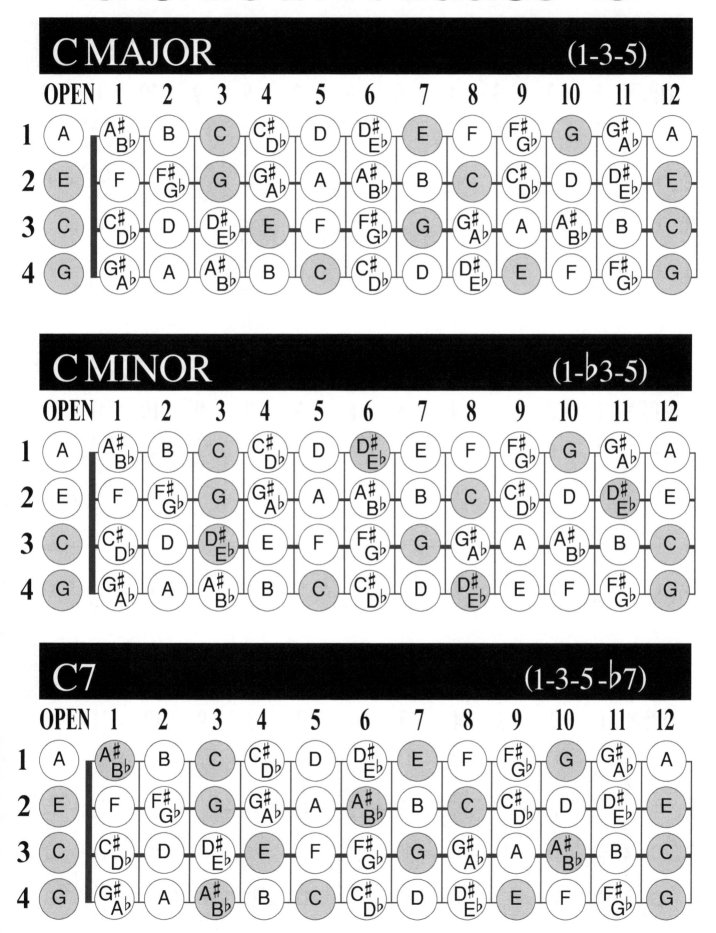

CHORDS & ARPEGGIOS - C♯ D♭

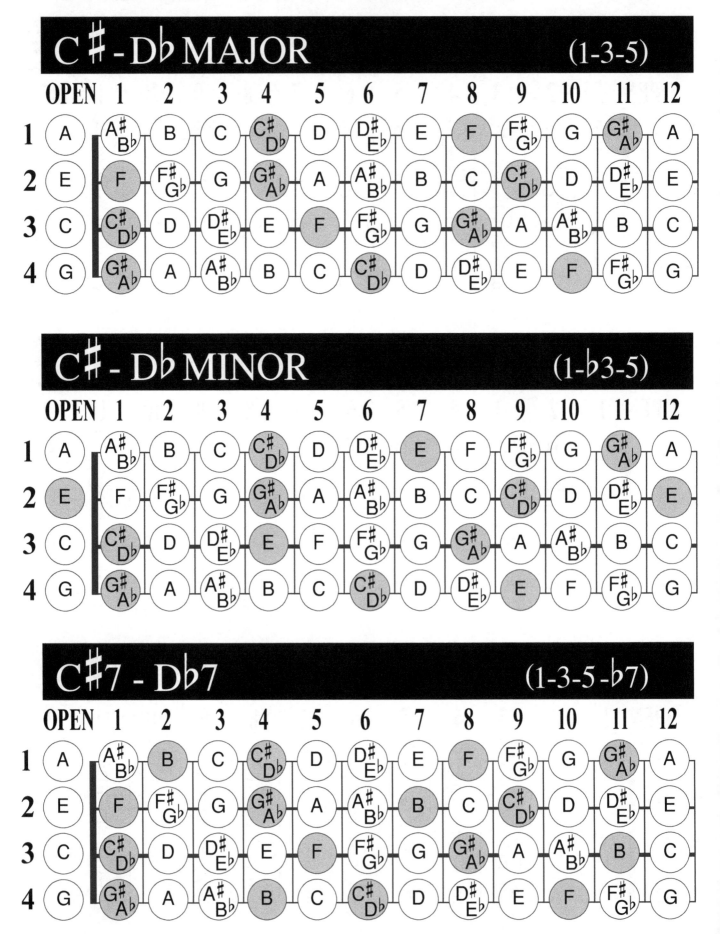

C♯ - D♭ MAJOR (1-3-5)

C♯ - D♭ MINOR (1-♭3-5)

C♯7 - D♭7 (1-3-5-♭7)

CHORDS & ARPEGGIOS - D

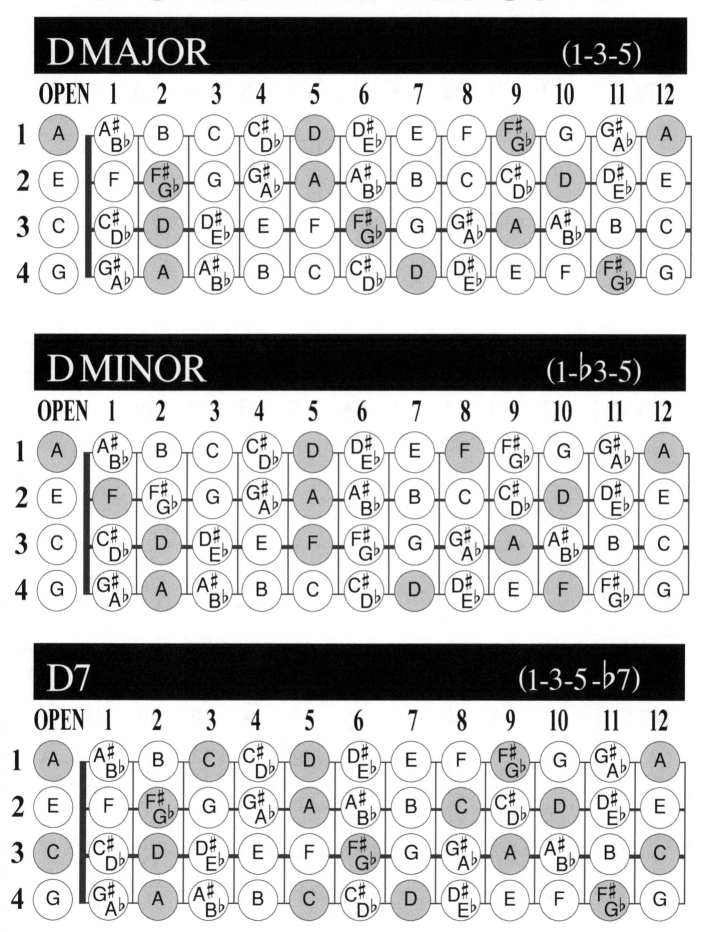

CHORDS & ARPEGGIOS - D# E♭

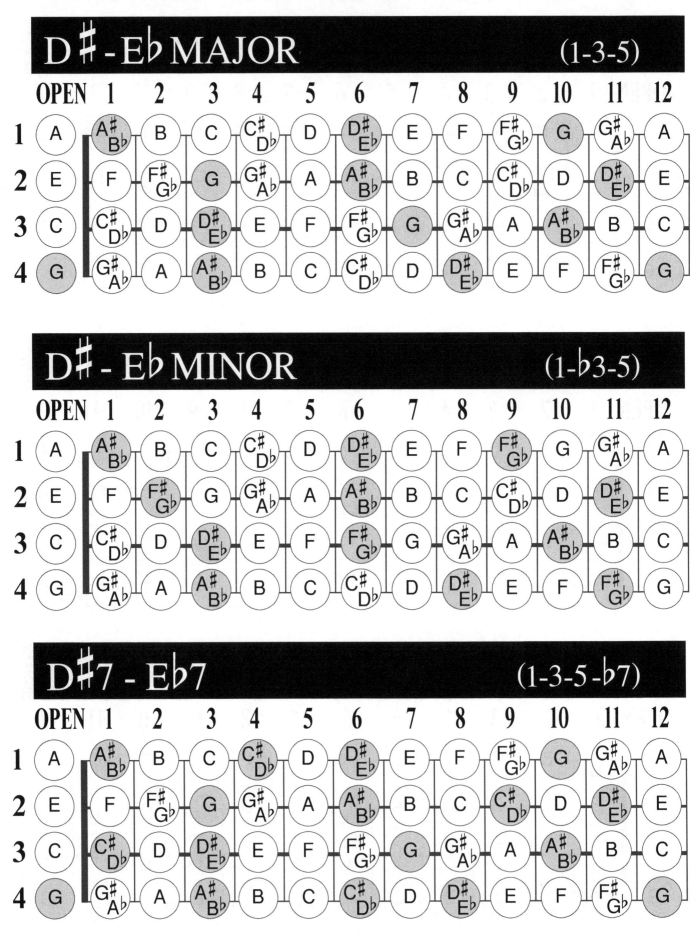

CHORDS & ARPEGGIOS - E

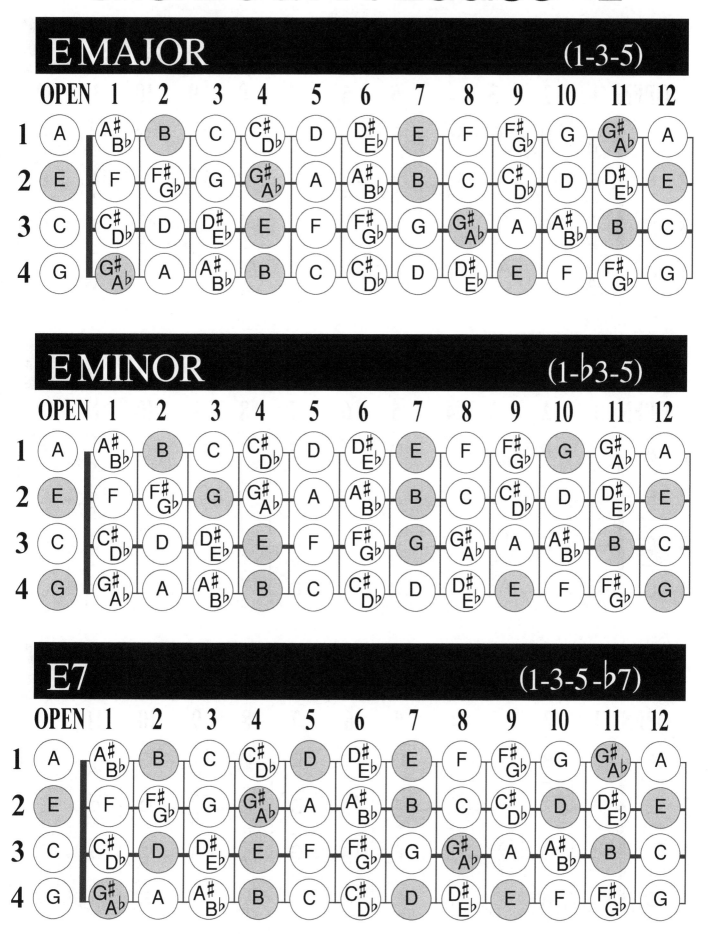

CHORDS & ARPEGGIOS - F

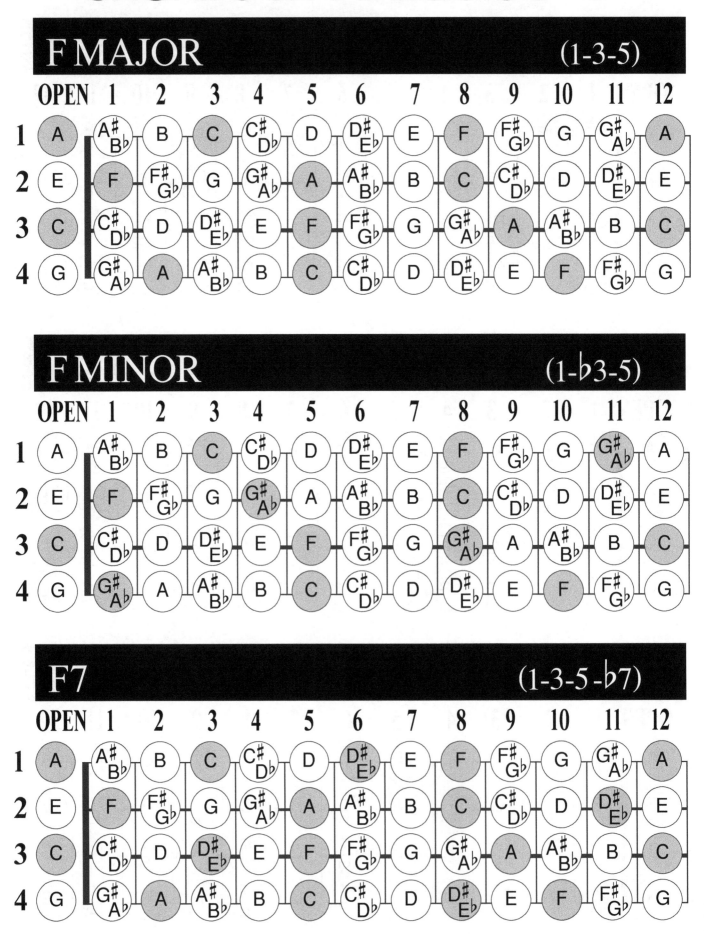

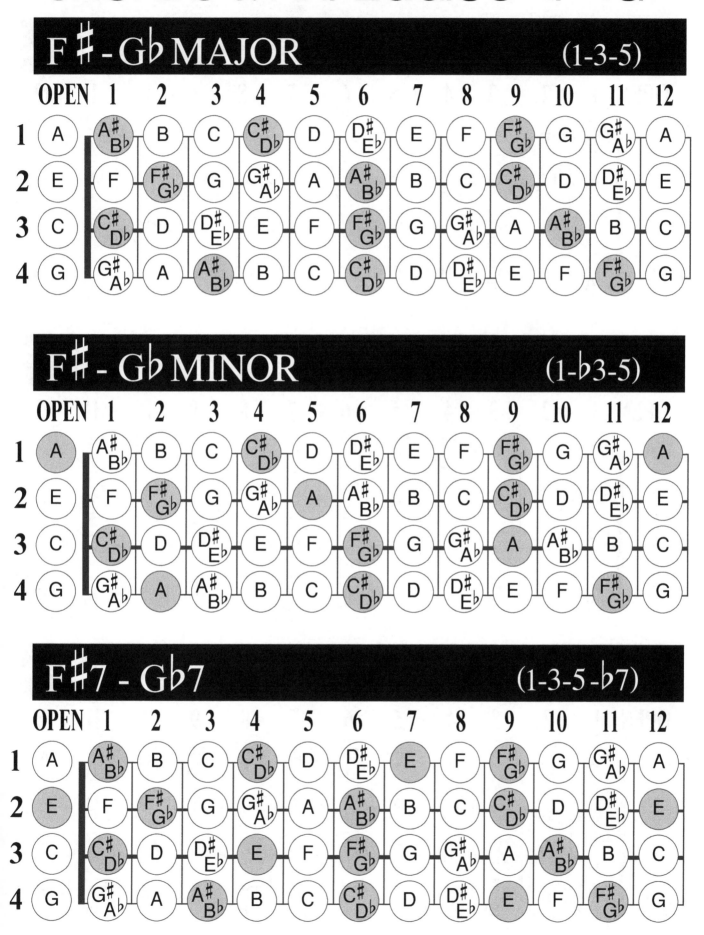

CHORDS & ARPEGGIOS - G

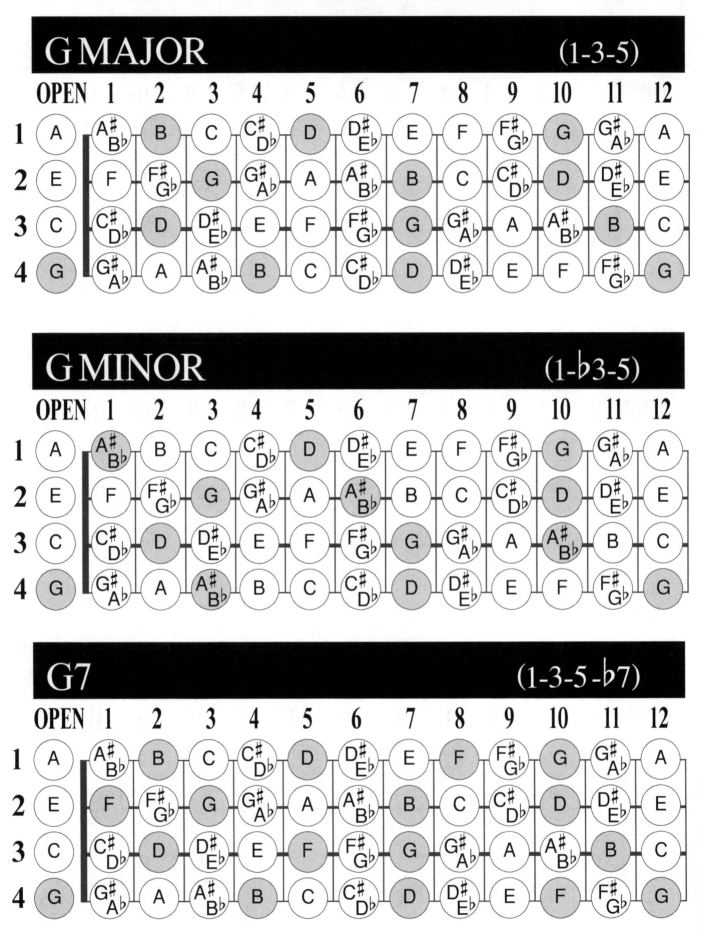

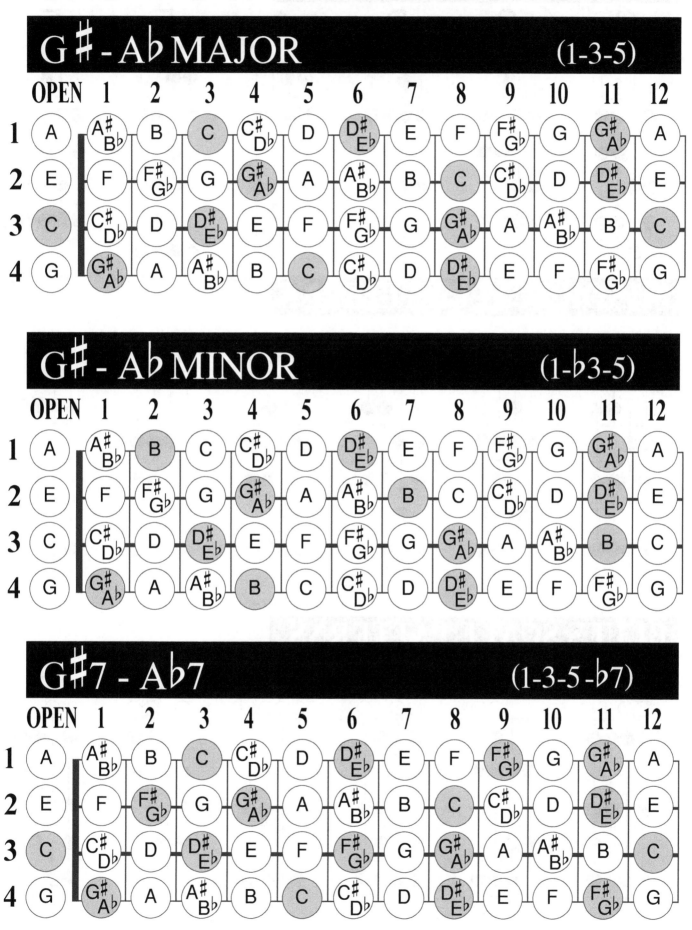

84

MAJOR SCALE PATTERNS

Root =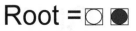

G

C
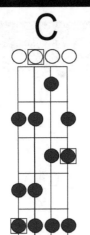

D
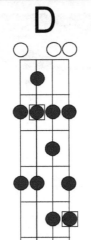

A
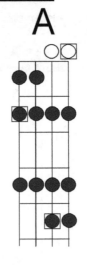

E
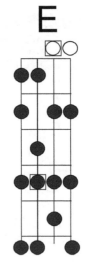

F
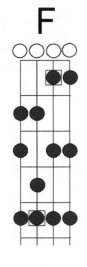

*Move all scales down one fret to play in all 12 keys

MINOR SCALE PATTERNS

Gm
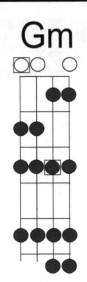

Bm
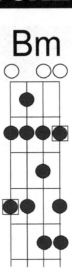

Dm
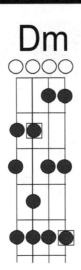

Am
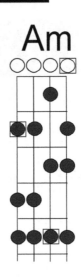

Em
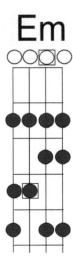

Fm
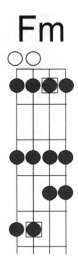

BLUES SCALE PATTERNS

G
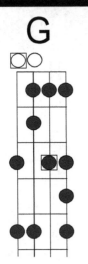

B
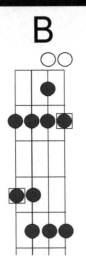

D
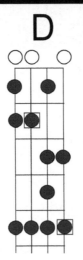

A

E
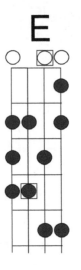

F
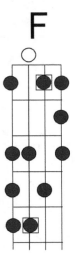

MIXOLYDIAN PATTERNS

Root = ☐ ⬛

G
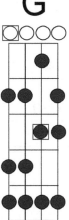

C
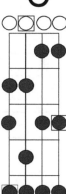

D
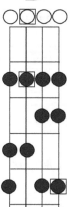

A
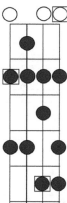

E
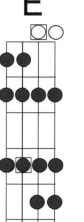

F
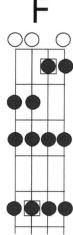

HARMONIC MINOR PATTERNS

Gm
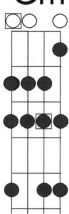

Bm
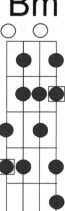

Dm
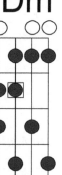

Am

Em
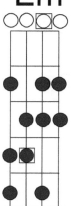

Fm
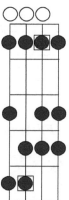

PENTATONIC MINOR

C
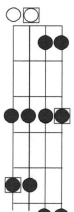

E
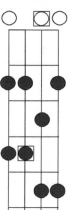

G
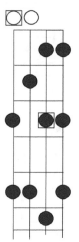

DIMINISHED-WHOLE TONE

DIMINISHED*   WHOLE TONE

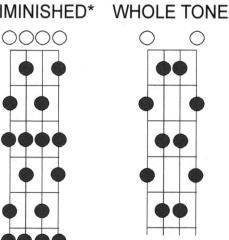

*Root can be any note

MAJOR SCALES
TUNING - G C E A

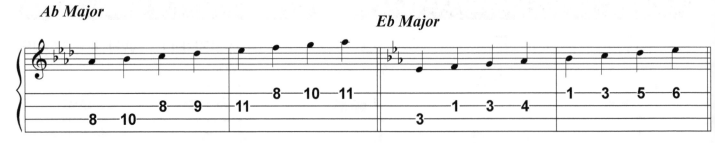

MINOR SCALES

BLUES SCALES

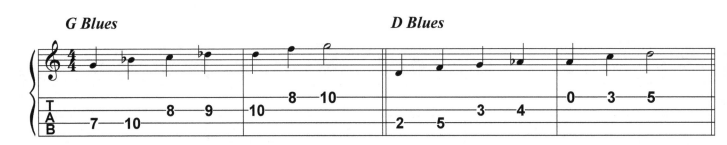

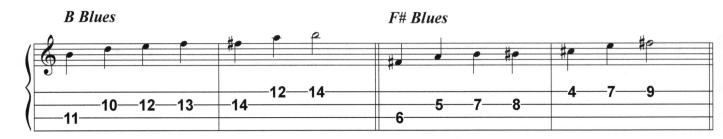

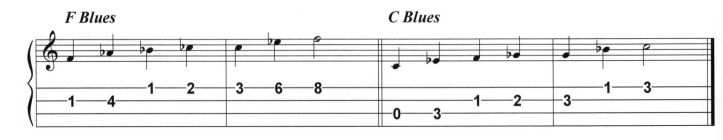

UKULELE NOTATION GUIDE

Downstroke
Pick down towards ground.

Upstroke
Pick up towards sky.

Accent
Strike the string harder to produce a louder sound.

Strong Accent (Martelato)
Pluck the string forcibly to produce a strong accent.

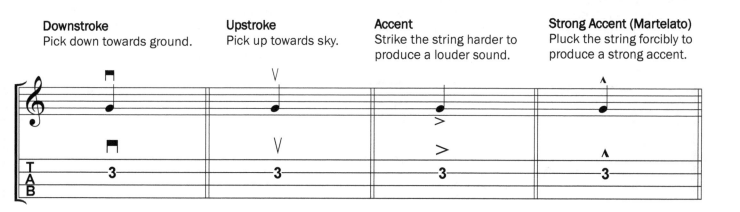

Staccato
Shorten note lenghth.

Accent with Staccato
Strike the string harder and let ring shorter. (Marcatto)

Tenuto
Slight accent. Hold note for full value.

Accent with Tenuto
Strike string harder and let ring for full value of note.

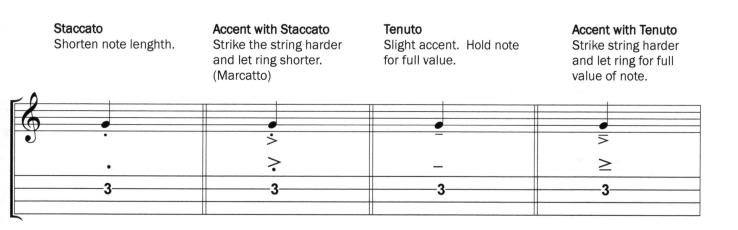

Hammer On
Play first note then hammer down finger without playing higher second note.

Pull Off
Play first note then grip on string and pull off to second lower note without playing.

Shift Slide
Slide finger/slide up or down to the next note on the same string. Pluck both notes.

Legato Slide
Slide finger/slide up or down to the next note on the same string.
Play only the first note.

Palm Muting (P.M.)
Place palm on strings near bridge to muffle the sound.

Left Hand Mute
Place left hand finger(s) on strings to mute sound. A percussive sound (x)

Grace Note
The smaller grace note is rhythmically combined with large note. Play quickly before larger note.

Ghost Note (Parenthesis)
An optional note or bracketed note played quickly before main note.

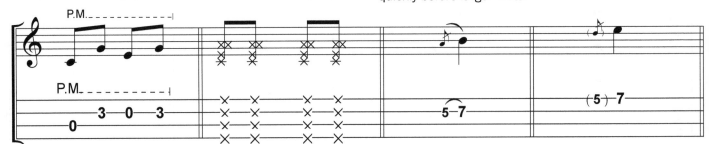

Vibrato
Bend string up and down. Can be slow or fast.

Wide Vibrato
Bend string up and down but with wider arc. Can be slow or fast.

Slight Bend
Slightly Bend the note up a 1/4 tone.

1/2 Tone Bend
Bend the note up a half tone or to sound 1 fret higher.

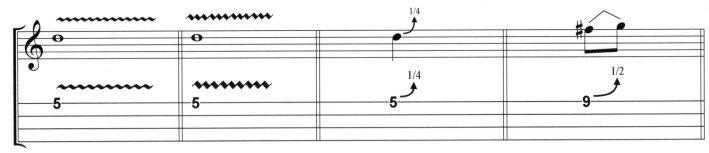

Whole Step Bend
Bend the note up a full whole tone or to sound 2 frets higher.

Bend and Release
Bend the note up and release back down to the original note.

Pre-Bend
Bend the note up then play note.

Pre-Bend
Bend the note up then play note.

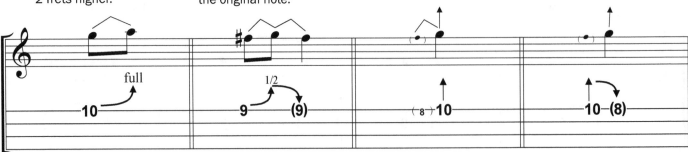

Hold Bend
Hold bend up until the end of the dashed line.

Multiple Bends
Several bends combined together.

Bend Neck
Grab headstock while holding body firm and bend neck.

Behind Nut Bend
Bend the string behind the nut at the headstock.

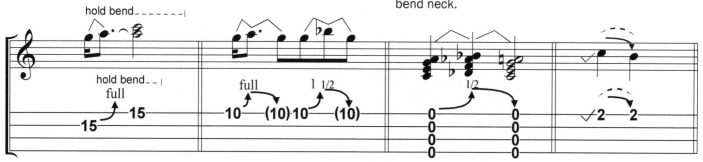

Rake
A percussive clicking sound before playing a note. Mute the strings (x) with the left hand. Often a muted arpeggio.

Arpeggiate
Strum the chord in the direction of the arrow.

Trill
Quickly alternate between two notes using hammer ons and pull offs.

Tapping (+)
Tap fret with finger or pick.

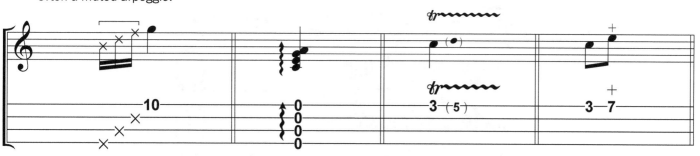

Natural Harmonic
Lightly place finger over fret indicated and pluck.

Artificial Harmonic
Hold done note indicated and lightly pluck pick finger higher up string with thumb.

Pick Slide (P.S.)
Place pick edge on string and scrape down or up string.

Tremelo Picking
Rapidly pick down and up on string.

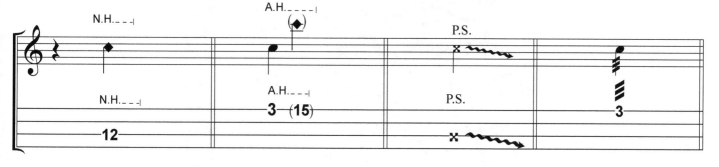

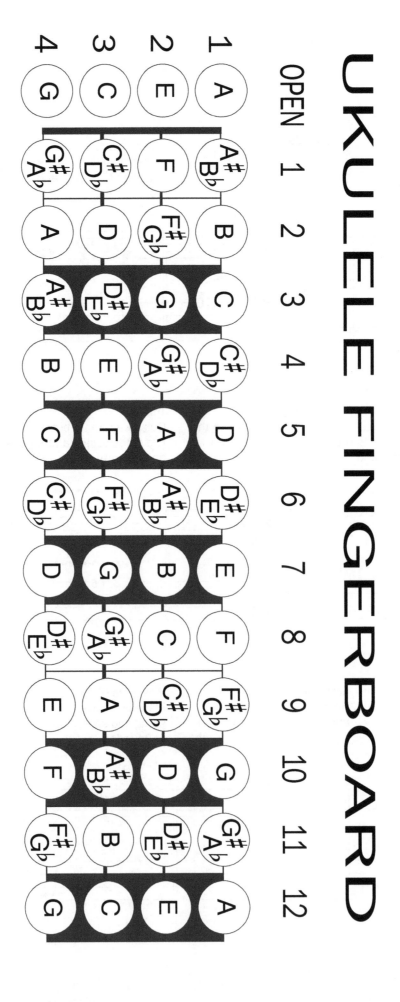

UKULELE FINGERBOARD

Ukulele Note Chart

1st String - A

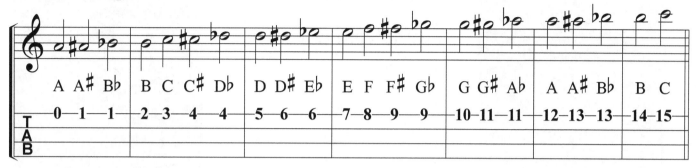

2nd String - E

3rd String - C

4th String - G

Also Available at www.KalymiMusic.com

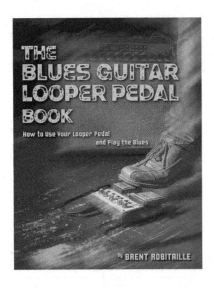

The Blues Guitar Looper
Pedal Book

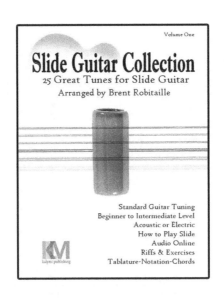

Slide Guitar Collection

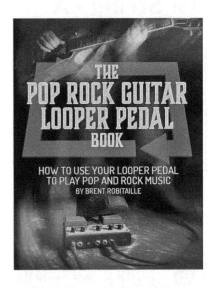

The Pop Rock Guitar
Looper Pedal Book

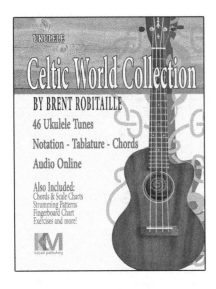

Celtic World Collection
Ukulele

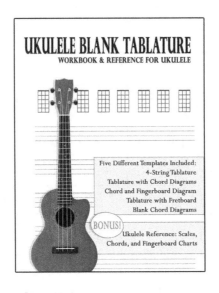

Ukulele Blank Tablature
Collection - Reference

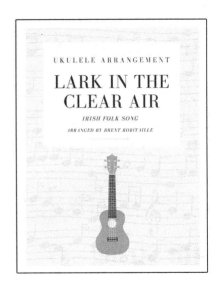

Ukulele Arrangements

GUITAR - CIGAR BOX GUITAR - MANDOLIN
UKULELE - VIOLIN - MUSIC BLOG - ARRANGEMENTS

Lightning Source UK Ltd.
Milton Keynes UK
UKHW051532011222
413201UK00021B/570